Francis Frith's
Yorkshire Dales

Photographic Memories

Francis Frith's
Yorkshire Dales

Roly Smith

First published in the United Kingdom in 2002 by
Frith Book Company Ltd

Paperback Edition 2002
ISBN 1-85937-502-2

British Library Cataloguing in Publication Data

Francis Frith's Yorkshire Dales
Roly Smith

Frith Book Company Ltd
Frith's Barn, Teffont,
Salisbury, Wiltshire SP3 5QP
Tel: +44 (0) 1722 716 376
Email: info@francisfrith.co.uk
www.francisfrith.co.uk

Printed and bound in Great Britain

Front Cover: Hawes, Haymaking 1924 H75754

AS WITH ANY HISTORICAL DATABASE THE FRITH ARCHIVE IS CONSTANTLY BEING CORRECTED AND IMPROVED
AND THE PUBLISHERS WOULD WELCOME INFORMATION ON OMISSIONS OR INACCURACIES

Contents

Francis Frith: *Victorian Pioneer*

FRANCIS FRITH, Victorian founder of the world-famous photographic archive, was a complex and multi-talented man. A devout Quaker and a highly successful Victorian businessman, he was both philosophic by nature and pioneering in outlook.

By 1855 Francis Frith had already established a wholesale grocery business in Liverpool, and sold it for the astonishing sum of £200,000, which is the equivalent today of over £15,000,000. Now a multi-millionaire, he was able to indulge his passion for travel. As a child he had pored over travel books written by early explorers, and his fancy and imagination had been stirred by family holidays to the sublime mountain regions of Wales and Scotland. 'What a land of spirit-stirring and enriching scenes and places!' he had written. He was to return to these scenes of grandeur in later years to 'recapture the thousands of vivid and tender memories', but with a different purpose. Now in his thirties, and captivated by the new science of photography, Frith set out on a series of pioneering journeys to the Nile regions that occupied him from 1856 until 1860.

Intrigue and Adventure

He took with him on his travels a specially-designed wicker carriage that acted as both dark-room and sleeping chamber. These far-flung journeys were packed with intrigue and adventure. In his life story, written when he was sixty-three, Frith tells of being held captive by bandits, and of fighting 'an awful midnight battle to the very point of surrender with a deadly pack of hungry, wild dogs'. Sporting flowing Arab costume, Frith arrived at Akaba by camel seventy years before Lawrence, where he encountered 'desert princes and rival sheikhs, blazing with jewel-hilted swords'.

During these extraordinary adventures he was assiduously exploring the desert regions bordering the Nile and patiently recording the antiquities and peoples with his camera. He was the first photographer to venture beyond the sixth cataract. Africa was still the mysterious 'Dark Continent', and Stanley and Livingstone's historic meeting was a decade into the future. The conditions for picture taking confound belief. He laboured for hours in his wicker dark-room in the sweltering heat of the desert, while the volatile chemicals fizzed dangerously in their trays. Often he was forced to work in remote tombs and caves where conditions were cooler. Back in London he exhibited his photographs and was 'rapturously cheered' by members of the Royal Society. His reputation as a photographer was made overnight. An eminent modern historian has likened their impact on the population of the time to that on our own generation of the first photographs taken on the surface of the moon.

Venture of a Life-Time

Characteristically, Frith quickly spotted the opportunity to create a new business as a specialist publisher of photographs. He lived in an era of immense and sometimes violent change. For the poor in the early part of Victoria's reign work was a drudge and the hours long, and people had precious little free time to enjoy themselves. Most had no transport other than a cart or gig at their disposal, and had not travelled far beyond the boundaries of their own town or village. However,

by the 1870s, the railways had threaded their way across the country, and Bank Holidays and half-day Saturdays had been made obligatory by Act of Parliament. All of a sudden the ordinary working man and his family were able to enjoy days out and see a little more of the world.

With characteristic business acumen, Francis Frith foresaw that these new tourists would enjoy having souvenirs to commemorate their days out. In 1860 he married Mary Ann Rosling and set out with the intention of photographing every city, town and village in Britain. For the next thirty years he travelled the country by train and by pony and trap, producing fine photographs of seaside resorts and beauty spots that were keenly bought by millions of Victorians. These prints were painstakingly pasted into family albums and pored over during the dark nights of winter, rekindling precious memories of summer excursions.

The Rise of Frith & Co

Frith's studio was soon supplying retail shops all over the country. To meet the demand he gathered about him a small team of photographers, and published the work of independent artist-photographers of the calibre of Roger Fenton and Francis Bedford. In order to gain some understanding of the scale of Frith's business one only has to look at the catalogue issued by Frith & Co in 1886: it runs to some 670 pages, listing not only many thousands of views of the British Isles but also many photographs of most European countries, and China, Japan, the USA and Canada – note the sample page shown above from the hand-written *Frith & Co* ledgers detailing pictures taken. By 1890 Frith had created the greatest specialist photographic publishing company in the world,

Frith's death, a new card measuring 5.5 x 3.5 inches became the standard format, but it was not until 1902 that the divided back came into being, with address and message on one face and a full-size illustration on the other. *Frith & Co* were in the vanguard of postcard development, and Frith's sons Eustace and Cyril continued their father's monumental task, expanding the number of views offered to the public and recording more and more places in Britain, as the coasts and countryside were opened up to mass travel.

Francis Frith died in 1898 at his villa in Cannes, his great project still growing. The archive he created continued in business for another seventy years. By 1970 it contained over a third of a million pictures of 7,000 cities, towns and villages. The massive photographic record Frith has left to us stands as a living monument to a special and very remarkable man.

with over 2,000 outlets – more than the combined number that Boots and W H Smith have today! The picture on the right shows the *Frith & Co* display board at Ingleton in the Yorkshire Dales. Beautifully constructed with mahogany frame and gilt inserts, it could display up to a dozen local scenes.

Postcard Bonanza

The ever-popular holiday postcard we know today took many years to develop. In 1870 the Post Office issued the first plain cards, with a pre-printed stamp on one face. In 1894 they allowed other publishers' cards to be sent through the mail with an attached adhesive halfpenny stamp. Demand grew rapidly, and in 1895 a new size of postcard was permitted called the court card, but there was little room for illustration. In 1899, a year after

Frith's Archive: *A Unique Legacy*

FRANCIS FRITH'S legacy to us today is of immense significance and value, for the magnificent archive of evocative photographs he created provides a unique record of change in 7,000 cities, towns and villages throughout Britain over a century and more. Frith and his fellow studio photographers revisited locations many times down the years to update their views, compiling for us an enthralling and colourful pageant of British life and character.

We tend to think of Frith's sepia views of Britain as nostalgic, for most of us use them to conjure up memories of places in our own lives with which we have family associations. It often makes us forget that to Francis Frith they were records of daily life as it was actually being lived in the cities, towns and villages of his day. The Victorian age was one of great and often bewildering change for ordinary people, and though the pictures evoke an impression of slower times, life was as busy and hectic as it is today.

We are fortunate that Frith was a photographer of the people, dedicated to recording the minutiae of everyday life. For it is this sheer wealth of visual data, the painstaking chronicle of changes in dress, transport, street layouts, buildings, housing, engineering and landscape that captivates us so much today. His remarkable images offer us a powerful link with the past and with the lives of our ancestors.

Today's Technology

Computers have now made it possible for Frith's many thousands of images to be accessed almost instantly. In the Frith archive today, each photograph is carefully 'digitised' then stored on a CD Rom. Frith archivists can locate a single photograph amongst thousands within seconds. Views can be catalogued and sorted under a variety of categories of place and content to the immediate benefit of researchers.

Inexpensive reference prints can be created for them at the touch of a mouse button, and a wide range of books and other printed materials assembled and published for a wider, more general readership - in the next twelve months over a hundred Frith local history titles will be published! The day-to-day workings of the archive are very different from how they were in Francis Frith's time: imagine the herculean task of sorting through eleven tons of glass negatives as Frith had to do to locate a particular sequence of pictures! Yet

See Frith at www.francisfrith.co.uk

the archive still prides itself on maintaining the same high standards of excellence laid down by Francis Frith, including the painstaking cataloguing and indexing of every view.

It is curious to reflect on how the internet now allows researchers in America and elsewhere greater instant access to the archive than Frith himself ever enjoyed. Many thousands of individual views can be called up on screen within seconds on one of the Frith internet sites, enabling people living continents away to revisit the streets of their ancestral home town, or view places in Britain where they have enjoyed holidays. Many overseas researchers welcome the chance to view special theme selections, such as transport, sports, costume and ancient monuments.

We are certain that Francis Frith would have heartily approved of these modern developments in imaging techniques, for he himself was always working at the very limits of Victorian photographic technology.

The Value of the Archive Today

Because of the benefits brought by the computer, Frith's images are increasingly studied by social historians, by researchers into genealogy and ancestory, by architects, town planners, and by teachers and schoolchildren involved in local history projects.

In addition, the archive offers every one of us an opportunity to examine the places where we and our families have lived and worked down the years. Highly successful in Frith's own era, the archive is now, a century and more on, entering a new phase of popularity.

The Past in Tune with the Future

Historians consider the Francis Frith Collection to be of prime national importance. It is the only archive of its kind remaining in private ownership and has been valued at a million pounds. However, this figure is now rapidly increasing as digital technology enables more and more people around the world to enjoy its benefits.

Francis Frith's archive is now housed in an historic timber barn in the beautiful village of Teffont in Wiltshire. Its founder would not recognize the archive office as it is today. In place of the many thousands of dusty boxes containing glass plate negatives and an all-pervading odour of photographic chemicals, there are now ranks of computer screens. He would be amazed to watch his images travelling round the world at unimaginable speeds through network and internet lines.

The archive's future is both bright and exciting. Francis Frith, with his unshakeable belief in making photographs available to the greatest number of people, would undoubtedly approve of what is being done today with his lifetime's work. His photographs, depicting our shared past, are now bringing pleasure and enlightenment to millions around the world a century and more after his death.

Yorkshire Dales - *An Introduction*

There are few scenes more instantly identifiable as English than the typical view of one of the Yorkshire Dales as seen from the moorland heights above. Take the view of Kettlewell in Wharfedale, for example. It shows the compact grey village, dominated by the tower of its medieval church, seeming to grow almost organically from the native rock on which it stands. It sits like a spider at the centre of an intricate web of dry stone walls spreading up the slopes of Langcliffe and Cam Head above, and every couple of enclosed meadows seem to have their own little gabled barn ready to take the summer's harvest of sweet-smelling, herb-rich hay.

In the valley bottom, where the swirling Wharfe is joined by Park Gill Beck, clumps of trees soften the scene. Above, on the fellsides, the native limestone breaks through the surface in the 'scars' of Langcliffe and Gate Cote. And in the background there is the constant backdrop of the brooding moors, leading up to the lonely summits of Cam Head and Great Whernside.

Some of the country's finest limestone and gritstone scenery make up the 638-square mile (1,769-sq km) Yorkshire Dales National Park - Britain's third largest after the Lake District and Snowdonia. Today's National Park, which was designed in 1954 and receives more than nine million annual visits, is, however, largely the creation of man, as the stone-walled fields and barns of the dales show.

The Rocks Beneath

Before man arrived on the scene, the Dales were a virgin landscape shaped by countless aeons of deposition, folding, faulting and erosion; given its final polish by the tremendous grinding power of Ice Age glaciers, the real architects of the dales themselves.

The bedrock of the Yorkshire Dales constitutes some of the oldest rocks known to man. The delicate pastel Ordovician slates exposed under the waterfalls of the Ingleton Glens have been estimated to be 500 million years old, and the celebrated 'unconformity' shown at Thornton Force is one of Britain's classic geological sites. The next oldest rocks are the Silurian slates, which make up the seductively smooth-sided Howgill Fells near Sedburgh in the north-west corner of the National Park. These are 440 million years old, and are geologically and physically much more closely aligned to the Lake District hills across the M6 motorway. But more than 90 per cent of the Yorkshire Dales National Park is made up of Carboniferous rocks, laid down under semi-tropical conditions around 300 million years ago, at a time when what we now know as Britain was much closer to the Equator.

The Yorkshire Dales represent one of the finest glacio-karst (limestone affected by glaciation) landscapes in Britain, and this was the prime reason for its designation as a national park. The central block of limestone, known as the Great Scar or Craven Limestone, stretches between Wharfedale in the east to beyond Ingleborough in the west, and is about 800 feet (244m) in depth. It is in this massively-bedded rock that the great scenic wonders of the Dales are found, such as the breathtaking 260ft (80m) high amphitheatre of Malham Cove, the awe-inspiring gorge of Gordale Scar, and the brooding overhang of Kilnsey Crag.

These were all carved by the awesome power of Ice Age glaciers, or by their rushing meltwaters. The tremendous natural planing effect of those same glaciers shaved off the surface soil to expose the so-called limestone pavements, with their intricate jigsaw of clints and grikes, so well seen above Malham Cove, on Moughton and on Southerscales Scar below Ingleborough.

It is within the shady and damp recesses of the grikes of the limestone pavements that some of the most beautiful botanical treasures of the Dales can be found. Here, in sheltered, greenhouse conditions, rare lime-loving plants such as hart's tongue fern, bloody cranesbill and lily of the valley flourish, safe from the biting wind and the nibbling teeth of sheep.

The other, often unseen, feature of limestone is the systems of potholes and caves which have been formed by underground streams and by the acidic effect of rainwater. The most famous of these are open to the public, such as the Ingleborough and White Scar Caves near Ingleton, and Stump Cross Caverns near Pateley Bridge in Nidderdale. Other true potholes, such as the huge maw of Gaping Gill - the largest open pothole in Britain - and Alum Pot on the slopes of Ingleborough, are strictly the preserve of cavers and potholers.

Many of the highest hills in the Yorkshire Dales, such as Ingleborough, Pen-y-Ghent, Penhill and Addleborough, have a distinctive stepped profile. The reason for this is that the later Carboniferous rocks were laid down in a sequence which is known as the Yoredale series, which takes its name from the old name for the River Ure of Wensleydale. The uppermost stratum of this series is a dark, abrasive sandstone, known as millstone grit from its former use for millstones. In the case of the highest peaks, this often forms a resistant cap over the earlier shales and limestones.

Millstone grit also predominates in the larger, poorly-drained areas of moorland above the dales, in which moorgrass and the fluffy white heads of cotton grass are among the few plants which can exist. Heather moorland is found in the slightly drier areas, such as Barden Fell and Barden Moor above Wharfedale.

The Coming of Man

First evidence of the arrival of Man is provided by the minute flint chippings which have been found on the highest moors. They show that as early as 10,000 years ago, these now inhospitable areas were being used in the summer by Mesolithic hunting parties, and the great clearance of the native wildwood had begun. (It is hard to believe, but apart from the very highest summits, most of today's moorland was once wooded, as well as the valley bottoms).

These earliest settlers left little to mark their passing, apart from those discarded flints, and the only other evidence of Stone Age man has been found in some of the more accessible caves such as Victoria Cave and the other caves in Attermire Scar, east of Settle. Elsewhere, only the enigmatic 'stone circle' at Yockenthwaite in Langstrothdale (which is more likely to be the enclosing kerb of a burial mound), and the Castle Dykes henge near Aysgarth between Bishopdale and Wensleydale, give any clue to their lifestyle.

It was during the Bronze and Iron Ages that farming really developed, and the words 'Celtic Fields' which we can still see on maps, especially around Grassington and Malham, show just how intensive that agriculture was. Still visible in aerial photographs or under the right lighting conditions are the fields, huts, cattle pounds, burial mounds and roadways of what must have been a large population of the people who became the first true dalesmen and women.

Easily the most impressive monument from the Iron Age is the magnificent hill fort of Ingleborough, which encircles the 2,372ft (723m) summit and is the highest in England. The 15-acre (6ha) enclosure contains the remains of a large number of hut circles, showing that in the summer months at least, a sizeable population lived within its massive stone walls.

The coming of the Romans established the classic dual economy of the Dales, which was to last for the next millennium and beyond. The riches of wool, hides and meat from the extensive grazing grounds of the dales was now to be supplemented by the exploitation of the hidden mineral wealth of the hills - in particular, lead. Pigs of lead dating from the reigns of Trajan and Hadrian have been discovered in the Dales, as the legions slowly infiltrated the hills from their base at York (Eboracum) in search of the precious but poisonous metal used in so much of their plumbing and roofing. But it was the next wave of invaders - the Saxons and the Vikings - who were to leave a much more lasting legacy.

We can still trace the spread of these barbarian hordes by studying the place-names on the map. To the east of the Dales, there is a distinct Danish influence in the place-names, which typically end in 'by'. But westwards, and into the lower reaches of the Dales, village names ending in 'ley' indicate a forest clearing made by the Anglians from the Low Countries around the Baltic.

West of this, in the higher reaches of the dales, the influence of the Norsemen is everywhere. They reached the area from Scotland and Ireland between the 9th and 11th centuries. Place-name elements like 'clint', 'beck', and 'foss' are all pure Norse, and sure indications that these high sheep pastures were first settled by Vikings and Norsemen, who must have felt more at home here. They also bred the archetypal Dalesmen - stern, independent free-thinkers who prefer to keep themselves to themselves.

The Norman invasion saw William the Conqueror's 'Harrying of the North', a systematic ethnic cleansing of the natives which was supervised from castles like those at Skipton,

Middleham and Richmond. Some of the deserted medieval village sites of the Dales date from this turbulent period; but many more market towns and villages of the Dales survived, and are still watched over by a medieval church tower or manor house.

It was during the Middle Ages that a more peaceful influence swept through the Dales in the form of the vast sheep ranches and granges run by the land-hungry monks of the great religious houses, such as those at Bolton Abbey in Wharfedale and Jervaulx in Wensleydale. The white-robed Cistercian monks gloried in their poverty, but paradoxically they were also great and highly successful entrepreneurs, and were among the first to build mills to harness the abundant water power of Dales rivers.

Water-powered industrialisation, which so dramatically altered the lower reaches of Dales rivers such as the Wharfe, the Aire and the Ouse during the 18th and 19th centuries, largely passed the Dales by. One industry, however, left lasting scars, especially in places like Swaledale and its subsidiary becks.

This was the lead which had first attracted the Romans, and places like Gunnerside Beck in Swaledale now have some of the finest remaining lead-based industrial archaeology in the country. The modern counterpart to lead mines are the huge limestone quarries which scar so many dalesides, but which provide an important source of local employment.

With the first railways which threaded the Dales - such as the 72-mile Settle to Carlisle railway built between 1869-76 - came the first tourists, to gape in wonder at attractions such as the Ingleton Glens, Kilnsey Crag and Malham Cove. The Settle - Carlisle line, with its 325 bridges, 21 viaducts, 14 tunnels and 21 stations, has been threatened with closure since Dr Beeching's day, but it was saved by a concerted campaign by local and national enthusiasts in the 1980s. Its most impressive monument is probably the soaring viaduct at Ribblehead, where the line is carried across the dale on 24 towering arches, with Ingleborough and Whernside standing sentinel over it.

Among the first tourists were the photographers sent by Francis Frith, who determined to faithfully record every village and town in the Dales, as well as the rest of the country. They found, as today's tourist still finds, a settled and largely peaceful landscape, despite all the changes through its long and varied history; a landscape not much changed from the days when the dual economies of farming and mining were still paramount.

This survey of Frith's photographs, which are mainly from the early 20th century, is split into two geographical sections: the Southern Dales, including Wharfedale, Malhamdale, Ribblesdale and the Ingleton area, and the Northern Dales, which encompass Wensleydale and Swaledale and their tributaries eastwards to Richmond.

◀ **Austwick
Main Street and the
Post Office c1955**
A135009
A cyclist pulls up to visit
Austwick's village Post
Office and general stores
on the left. In the
background is the
apsidal end of the
Victorian parish church
of the Epiphany, with the
war memorial in front.

The Southern Dales

◄ **Arncliffe
The River and the
Bridge c1955** A132002
A flotilla of ducks form
the foreground to this
photograph of Arncliffe's
elegant bridge over the
River Skirfare. Originally
medieval, the bridge is a
major feature of the
attractive little village
which is the main
settlement in Littondale,
a valley which branches
off Wharfedale.

◄ **Bolton Abbey
From the Falls c1885**
18503
This is a splendid view of
the ruins of Bolton
Abbey (which is really a
priory) from the Falls,
overlooking the River
Wharfe. A popular place
for the citizens of
Bradford and Leeds,
Bolton Abbey is famous
for its stepping stones
across the river, which
are just out of shot at the
bottom of this picture.

▼ **Bolton Abbey, From the North-East c1885** 18517
This is the ruined chancel of the Augustinian priory at Bolton Abbey, which was
founded in 1155 and flourished until the Dissolution of the Monasteries by Henry
VIII in 1539. Fortunately, the nave of the church was retained as the parish church
for the village, which is part of the Duke of Devonshire's Yorkshire estate.

▼ **Bolton Abbey, Bolton Bridge 1923** 74502
A pair of Shorthorn cows rest contentedly in the flood meadows by the River
Wharfe at Bolton Abbey, just downstream from the bridge across the river. The
busy A59 road from Skipton to Harrogate crosses the river at this point, where
Ferry House is thought to stand on the site of a former chapel.

▲ **Buckden
The Village c1955**
B347031
In this charming
photograph, a collie
sheepdog marshals a
flock of white-nosed
Swaledale sheep past the
village green at Buckden.
In the background are the
limestone scars which
mark the lower slopes of
Buckden Pike, at 2,302
feet a notable viewpoint
in Upper Wharfedale.

◀ **Burnsall**
The Village 1926 79075
The ivy-clad Red Lion at Burnsall is the main hostelry in this central Wharfedale village, which clusters around its tidy village green sheltering under Burnsall Fell. It remains a predominately farming village, although tourism is now probably of equal importance.

Burnsall
The Bridge 1926
79076
Perhaps the best-known feature of Burnsall is its magnificent, five-arched stone bridge across the River Wharfe, seen here from the river. Originally built by Sir William Craven to link the village with Appletreewick, it has been rebuilt several times and is the only crossing in a six-mile length of the river.

Chapel Le Dale, Weathercote Cave 1890 23862
Weathercote Cave, below the Hill Inn at Chapel le Dale in Ribblesdale, is a typical Dales pothole
on the lower slopes of Whernside, the highest of the Dales' famous Three Peaks. The powerful
waterfalls drops 65 feet into the pothole behind the wedged boulder (seen here in the centre),
which is known by the curious name of Mohammed's Coffin.

Clapham, The Village c1950 C109024
This photograph shows a steeply-sloping green in Clapham, the picturesque Ribblesdale village which is a popular starting point for the ascent of Ingleborough, at 2,375ft perhaps the best known of the Three Peaks.

Clapham, Broken Bridge 1900 45772
Broken Bridge, in the centre of Clapham, crosses the fast-flowing Clapham Beck, which rises at Ingleborough Cave higher up the valley. It is a narrow structure now used by walkers, but like many Dales bridges, it was originally designed for use by trains of packhorses.

Clapham, The Entrance to Ingleborough Cave c1950 C109003
Here we see the low arched entrance to Ingleborough Cave, one of the major show caverns
of the Yorkshire Dales. The rocks just inside the entrance were blasted out by the owner in
1837 to drain an underground lake and gain access to a fine cavern draped with
stalagmites and stalactites.

Clapham, Ingleborough Cave c1950 C109002
Looking out from inside, we are in the iron-gated entrance passage of Ingleborough Cave. This is the section which was dynamited in 1837 to open out the show-cave now so popular with visitors who have to walk a mile up from the village to reach it.

Conistone, Springtime c1960 C725010
A shepherd and his faithful dog round up a flock of sheep and their new-born lambs in this springtime shot taken at Conistone-with-Kilnsey, a small village which consists of two hamlets on either side of the upper valley of the River Wharfe. Note the sturdy, stone-built barns and the upended cart on the right of the photograph.

Cowling
The View from Hallam Hill c1960 C269005
Cowling is a moorland parish in the Aire Valley about six miles south of Skipton. It once boasted several woollen mills - we can see their chimneys in this view. Cowling was also famous as a pioneer in commercial poultry keeping in the early years of the 20th century.

▼ **Draughton, The Village c1955** D259003

Draughton (pronounced 'Drafton') lies on the Craven Fault on the eastern bank of the River Wharfe. This general view of the village shows the village green (centre) with the whitewashed gable end of the café on the right-hand side in the middle distance.

▼ **Gargrave, The Square c1955** G105001

A view of the village square at Gargrave today would be dominated by parked cars, but when this photograph was taken in the mid-Fifties, it was empty apart from the village war memorial. Note the village ladies suspiciously eyeing the photographer outside the village café, and the little girl with her doll's pram on the right.

▲ **Giggleswick The Village 1887** 20413

The strangely-named Tems Beck, seen here in a culverted section, flows through Giggleswick and into the River Ribble. A notable feature of some of the older houses in Giggleswick are their date stones, usually found over the doorways of the village cottages, like those seen in the background of this picture.

◀ **Giggleswick**
Gigaleswick School,
The Chapel 1903 50146
Gigaleswick School, one of
the most famous public
schools in Yorkshire, was
originally founded as a
chantry by James Carr, and
was granted a Royal Charter
by Edward VI as early as
1553. The copper dome of
the chapel, built on a rocky
crag by Walter Morrison to
commemorate the Diamond
Jubilee of Queen Victoria in
1897, is a notable local
landmark.

**Grassington
The Market Square
1926** 79058
The cobbled Market
Square at Grassington
at a time when early
charabancs, like that on
the left of the photograph,
still vied with horses and
carts, like that seen in the
centre background under
the tree. Local buses are
parked in front of the
shops, awaiting their
passengers.

◀ **Greenhow Hill The Organ, Stump Cross Cavern c1955**
G118001
A guide points out the stalactite formation known as the Organ in Stump Cross Cavern, one of the Dales' popular show-caves, at Greenhow Hill on the Pateley Bridge to Grassington Road. Like many caverns, it was discovered by local lead miners when they were prospecting for the precious ore.

◄ **Grassington**
The Bridge 1900 45776
The embanked and buttressed stone bridge over the fast-flowing River Wharfe just outside Grassington is a prominent local landmark on the road to Threshfield, and on the road which runs north up the western side of the dale to Kilnsey and Kettlewell.

▼ **Hellifield**
Gisburn Road c1955
H493006
A touring cyclist has the road to himself as he passes through the sunlit village of Hellifield, a Ribblesdale village which only came into being in the late 19th century when the Lancashire and Yorkshire and London, Midland and Scottish Railways joined just north of here.

◄ **High Bentham**
Station Road c1950
H518016
High Bentham, on the banks of the River Wenning, was another village made more important by its railway station, which served the popular tourist honeypot of Ingleton, a couple of miles to the north. It has a twin neighbour in Low Bentham. Note the traffic-free street and curious onlookers.

▼ **Horton-in-Ribblesdale, The Village 1921** 71354
Here we see the narrow bridge over the infant River Ribble at Horton-in-Ribblesdale, in the centre of Yorkshire's Three Peaks country. Note the gateposts strangely marooned in the middle of the river, and the two out-houses, probably pig sties, in the gardens of the cottages on the right.

▼ **Hubberholme, The View from the Bridge c1950** H130004
The charmingly-named village of Hubberholme lies on the banks of the River Wharfe at the entrance to Langstrothdale. It is thought to take its name, like so many of these higher Dales villages, from an early Norse settler, in this case 'Hunburgh'. In the background of this view from the bridge, the dazzling-white limestone scars stand out on the surrounding fells.

▲ **Ingleton**
General View 1890
26327
The parish church of St Mary can be seen in the centre, and the now disused railway viaduct of the Midland Railway, erected in 1885, is on the extreme right of this general view.

◄ **Ingleton**
The Main Street 1926
79130
Mrs Fell appeared to be putting up new curtains in the top gable window (top left) of their café property in the centre of Ingleton when this photograph was taken. Interested bystanders in the distance down the Main Street watch the Frith photographer.

◄ **Ingleton
Thornton Foss 1887**
20428
The mighty Thornton
Foss (or Force) is the
highlight of the
celebrated Ingleton
Glens waterfalls walk.
This is where the River
Twiss crashes 65 feet
over a lip of limestone
which is bedded over
upturned beds of
incredibly-ancient
Precambrian slates at
one of the most
celebrated geological
showplaces in Britain.

◀ **Ingleton**
Thornton Church
1926 79157
A sheepdog poses obligingly as it herds its flock of Swaledale sheep in front of the lych-gate of the parish church in the hamlet of Thornton-in-Lonsdale, which lies just to the west of Ingleton.

▼ **Kettlewell**
General View 1900
45799
The charming village of Kettlewell is the gem of mid-Wharfedale, standing at the junction of the river with Park Gill Beck, which dashes down from the heights of Great Whernside to the east. This general view shows the village nestling comfortably amid the stone-walled fells.

◀ **Kettlewell**
The Beck 1900 45804
A beautiful view of Park Gill Beck as its waters cascade over the shelves of limestone to the east of Kettlewell. A typical stone-built Dales barn stands in the middle distance, with the limestone scars of Langcliffe behind.

▼ **Kettlewell, The Race Horses Hotel c1955** K14012
The Race Horses Hotel in the centre of Kettlewell is a typical Dales public house; its stone walls are rendered and painted white, it has gritstone tiles on the roof, and what remains of an archway through to stables at the rear, on the right.

▼ **Kilnsey, Kilnsey Crag c1900** K71307
The most striking feature of Kilnsey village in Upper Wharfedale is the great hooded cowl of Kilnsey Crag, seen here on the right. The notched overhang marks precisely the height of the last Ice Age glacier which swept down and shaped the valley as we see it today. Victorian children pose for the cameraman. Note the sign for stabling on the wall on the left.

▲ **Langcliffe
The Village 1895** 35221
Langcliffe is a typical Dales village lying about a mile north of Settle. The village is centred on its large, circular green, seen in the centre of the photograph. The Victorian village church is set slightly apart from the village, and can be seen in the trees at bottom right.

◀ **Linton**
The Village c1955 L171002
Solid stone-built cottages
and barns surround the
rectangular village green of
Linton, which slopes down
to the railed-off Linton Beck
which is crossed by three
bridges, one of which is
seen here on the right, and
a ford.

◀ **Linton**
Haytime c1955 L171017
A wonderful period photograph of hay-making near Linton in Wharfedale. Drawn by two faithful Dales-bred ponies, the farmer sits on his cutter as it slices through the sweet-smelling hay crop which will keep his stock through the bitter Dales winter.

◄ **Linton**
The Stepping Stones
1900 45784

The four-storey cotton and worsted mill in background of this photograph of the River Wharfe at Linton-in-Craven, near Grassington, has long been demolished, but the weir and stepping stones remain. Originally a water mill, all that remains of the centuries-old industry are two rows of cottages known as 'Botany'.

▼ **Long Preston**
The Fountain and the
Memorial c1965 L168024

Long Preston, spread on either side of the busy A65 Skipton to Kirkby Lonsdale road, retains a peaceful air. The Maypole Hotel (left) stands on the village green, alongside the Victorian Fountain (foreground) and war memorial (right).

◄ **Malham**
The Village c1910
M139020

The network of limestone walls which enmesh the fells surrounding the pretty Airedale village of Malham are well seen in the background of this photograph, taken on the banks of the river. The whitewashed hotel in the centre of the photograph was serving the early tourists to this scenic showplace, still a major Dales honeypot.

Malham, A Sheep Sale on the Green c1910 M139023
The village green at Malham was the scene of regular sheep sales
attended by farmers from the surrounding fells at the time when
this photograph was taken. The crammed pens full of white-nosed
Swaledale sheep are critically inspected by the bowler-hatted
farmers, who would undoubtedly haggle over the price they
expected to get or pay.

Malham, The River and the Bridge c1960 M139100
A touring cyclist leaves his machine leaning on the walls of the narrow bridge over the infant Aire in Malham while he consults his map. Perhaps he had just called at the Post Office and General Store, just over the bridge in the centre of the photograph.

Malham, Malham Cove c1877 9470
The great scenic wonder of Malham is the soaring, 260-foot amphitheatre of Malham Cove, just to the north of the village. This huge cliff of Carboniferous limestone was the scene of a waterfall higher than Niagara at the end of the Ice Age, but water seldom trickles over it today.

Malham, Gordale Scar c1881 13663
The other great geological showplace of Malham is the awesome cleft of Gordale Scar, seen here from inside its narrow, claustrophobic walls, looking out along the bed of Gordale Beck. The gorge was formed by the erosive waters of the beck when it was swelled by meltwaters at the end of the last Ice Age.

Settle, From the West 1924 75787
The little market town of Settle stands on the River Ribble, and is a centre for the central southern Dales. It is seen here from the west, with Sugar Loaf Hill prominent on the skyline and the viaduct of the Settle to Carlisle Railway in the middle distance.

Settle, The Market Place 1887 20403
It must have been a Monday when this charming photograph was taken, because it shows the Market Place at Settle hung-out with washing from the cottages above the Market Hall. Note the sign at the left-hand end of the building, which advertises 'S. Taylor Clog and Patten Maker', and the limestone crag of Castlebergh behind.

Settle
The Market Place
c1955 S97026
An interesting contrast is shown in this mid-Fifties view of the Market Place, this time on a Tuesday when the weekly market was in full swing. The biggest change is obviously the cars, now parked all down the main street. Note the old-style petrol pumps on the extreme left.

Settle, The Ebbing and Flowing Well 1921 71326
Like many villages founded on limestone, Settle has its Ebbing and Flowing Well. This is a spring which issues from the limestone as it hits impervious rocks beneath the limestone, ebbing and flowing as the water flow dictates.

Settle, Attermire Rocks 1887 20408
A contented herd of Shorthorn cattle graze peacefully in front of the rugged limestone scars of Attermire Scars or Rocks, which are situated about a mile to the east of Settle on the side of Langcliffe Scar. The scar is riddled with caves, and at Victoria Cave, some of the earliest evidence of Man in the Dales was found.

Skipton, The Castle Gateway 1900 45759
Skipton is probably best known for its castle, originally built by the
Norman Robert de Romile but largely rebuilt in the 14th to 17th
centuries. This view shows the imposing twin drum-towered
gateway, thought to date from the late 12th or early 13th century,
and built by the Cliffords, whose coat of arms and motto
'Desormais' (meaning 'Henceforth') are above the entrance.

**Skipton
The High Street 1900**
45757
If Settle is the capital of
the central southern
dales, then the ancient
market town of Skipton
is the centrepiece of the
eastern half. This
beautiful view of
Skipton's cobbled High
Street shows horses and
carts filling the street,
while the Perpendicular
tower of the 14th-
century parish church
of the Holy Trinity
watches over the scene.

▼ **Skipton, The High Street and the War Memorial 1911** 63580c
Another view of the High Street, showing the white column of the war memorial in the distance, to the right of the tower of the church. By now, motorised traffic has well and truly taken the place of the horses and carts of picture 45757, but cyclists could still ride on the wrong side of the road with impunity!

▼ **Stainforth, The Bridge 1921** 71346
The graceful single-arch bridge over the River Ribble at Stainforth links the main village with Little Stainforth to the west. Now cared for by the National Trust, the bridge is thought to be originally medieval in construction.

▲ **Starbotton
The Village 1926** 79083
A quiet corner of Starbotton, two miles from Kettlewell in Wharfedale, showing the Cam Gill Beck which enters the Wharfe from the slopes of Great Whernside, in the centre of the village. Most of the cottages in Starbotton, like those seen here, date from the 17th century.

◄ **Threshfield**
The Stocks and the Old
Hall c1955 T131012
The Old Hall Inn at
Threshfield in Upper
Wharfedale dates back to
the late 18th century, and
stands on what is left of the
village green, complete with
its stocks. The centre of
Threshfield lies away from
the main road between
Skipton and Kilnsey, and
remains relatively unspoilt.

THE NORTHERN DALES

Arkengarthdale c1960 R238040
Arkengarthdale is a little-visited but very beautiful
dale which runs into Swaledale from the north-west
at Reeth. It was formed by the Arkle Beck, which
rises high on Sleightholme Moor and passes
through some lovely hamlets such as Arkle Town,
Whaw and Langthwaite in typical Dales countryside.

Askrigg
General View 1911
63465
This general view of Askrigg's market square was taken from the tower of the church of St Oswald. The market cross in picture 20372 (page 58) is slightly hidden by the tree in the left foreground, but the delightful situation of the village among the surrounding Wensleydale fells can be appreciated.

Askrigg, The Street 1887 20372
The stone-stepped ancient market cross watches over Askrigg's market square as it has for over 500 years. Stately three-storied town houses, mainly dating from the 18th century, line the square in this village, which was once the 'capital' of Wensleydale.

Askrigg
Mill Gill Foss 1896 38302
Mill Gill Foss ('foss' is an Old Norse name for a waterfall) tumbles gracefully over a lip of limestone near the village. These falls have attracted visitors for centuries, starting with William Turner and William Wordsworth, and as early as 1908, the mill at their foot was used to provide electricity for the village.

Aysgarth, The Village and the War Memorial 1924 75720
Aysgarth is a tidy little village in central Wensleydale carrying a
name which gives away its Norse origins. The newly-erected war
memorial honouring the dead of the First World War is seen here
on the left.

**Aysgarth
The Steps to the Lower
Falls 1909** 61755
Aysgarth is perhaps best
known for its spectacular
series of waterfalls where
the River Ure dashes
spectacularly over a series
of resistant shelves of
limestone in the riverbed.
This photograph shows
the well-worn limestone
steps which led tourists
down to the Lower Falls
for many years.

▼ **Aysgarth, The Bridge and the Upper Falls 1909** 61765
This photograph, taken at the same time as 61755, gives a glimpse of the Upper Falls
at Aysgarth, seen through the sweeping arch of the sturdy village bridge. The falls
are now reached by a series of engineered paths and viewpoints, constructed by
the Yorkshire Dales National Park Authority.

▲ **Bainbridge
The Green 1906** 56025
The most important
feature of the mid-
Wensleydale village of
Bainbridge is its extensive
village green. There
appears to have been
some kind of show taking
place when Frith's
photographer called,
judging from the large
white marquee on the
green in the right of the
photograph. Note too the
horses grazing on the
green in the centre.

◄ **Bainbridge
The Rose and Crown
1929** 82604
This is a close-up of the
Rose and Crown public
house at Bainbridge, which
can be seen in the distance
in the centre of photograph
56025. This comfortable
hostelry overlooks
Bainbridge's spacious village
green, and some customers
can be seen sitting outside
admiring the view.

▼ Bainbridge, The Falls 1909 61769

Bainbridge, like so many Dales villages in this land of waterfalls, has its own series, seen here from the village bridge. Note the stepped nature of the river bed, formed because of the different levels of erosion resistance in the various limestones, which in turn creates the shallow, almost semi-circular, falls.

▼ Bellerby, The Village and the Church 1914 67229

Bellerby is a small village to the north of Leyburn in lower Wensleydale. This view shows the centre of the village, with the small Victorian parish church with its detached spire on the right.

▲ Bellerby Barden Moor 1929

82577

This remote dry stone-walled road leads north-east out of Bellerby past Halfpenny House, seen here in the middle distance, over Barden Moor and down eventually into Richmond in Swaledale by Waithwith Bank.

◀ **Carperby**
The Village 1909 61763
A tree was planted on the green in 1897 to mark Queen Victoria's Diamond Jubilee, and in the middle distance on the right we can see the remains of an ancient market cross set on seven square steps dated 1674.

◄ **Castle Bolton**
The Castle from the
North-East 1911 63475
Sir Richard Scope's
formidable 14th-century
castle at Castle Bolton
commands extensive
views over his estates in
lower Wensleydale, as this
view from the north east
shows. Although it was
slighted by Cromwell's
forces after a year-long
siege in 1644-5, the
substantial ruins are still
impressive, and open to
the public.

◄ **Carperby**
The Village 1929 82570
Here we have another view of Carperby's village green showing the market cross in the background. Two little girls pose obligingly for the camera. The village had its own market until the 14th century, when neighbouring Askrigg took over in 1587, although it appears that Carperby's market was revived again in the 17th century.

▼ **Castle Bolton**
The Museum 1911
63481
The small museum at Castle Bolton gives some idea of the enormous wealth and influence of the Scropes. It has a collection of some of the most important artefacts which have been found locally and which are associated with the castle.

◄ **Castle Bolton**
The Post Office c1955
C42003
The ivy-clad Post Office at Castle Bolton occupied a typical Dales cottage, but one which had an unusual apsidal end, on the left. The seat in the foreground looks as though it has seen better days, and might not take the weight of too many visitors!

◄ **Catterick
Richmond Road c1955**
C50033
Richmond Road runs
through the centre of
Catterick village. Note the
two soldiers marching down
the road side by side in the
centre of the photograph,
just to the right of Craster's
corner shop.

◄ **Catterick**
The Bridge House Hotel
c1950 C50008
Catterick Bridge, on the old A1 Great North Road, is about half a mile away from Catterick village and its associated army garrison. This view shows the bridge over the River Swale on the right, the Bridge House Hotel, centre, and a local man who appears to be washing something in the river.

▼ **Catterick**
The Camp, Kemmel Lines
c1955 C50045
Mention Catterick to most people and they will immediately think of the great army garrison, which is actually situated four miles from the village itself. The camp was recommended by Lord Baden Powell in 1911, and since then, thousands of 'squaddies', like these seen on marching drill at Kemmel Lines, have passed through.

◄ **Catterick**
The Camp Canteen,
Sandes Soldiers' Home
c1960 C50070
An army marches on its stomach, and all soldiers have to be well fed; those stationed at Catterick are no exception. This photograph shows men and some nurses taking refreshment in the canteen at Sandes Soldiers' Home. Typically, some of the squaddies seem to be more interested in the nurses than in the NAAFI food.

**Coverdale
Drovers' Crag 1926**
79050
The Yorkshire Dales are criss-crossed by a network of ancient drovers' roads, like this one in Coverdale, a quiet dale which runs into the lower reaches of Wensleydale. They are usually characterised by their width: large herds of cattle, sometimes from as far away as Scotland, were driven down them by generations of drovers to markets in the lowlands.

▼ **East Witton, The Village c1960** E78004

The large glacial boulder seen here at the bottom end of East Witton's spacious village green was brought here by a team of 20 horses from a field on the Cover Bridge road in 1859. It then served as the location of one of the three taps on the green which were the only water supply to the villagers until the mains supply arrived.

▼ **East Witton, The Church 1918** 68199

A disastrous fire in 1796 devastated the village of East Witton, at the eastern entrance to Wensleydale. When rebuilding took place in the early 19th century, the parish church of St John the Evangelist replaced the old church of St Martins. This is a view of the west tower.

▲ **Fremington The Bridge c1960**

F239025

The fine, three-arched buttressed bridge at Fremington, just outside Reeth in Swaledale, has spanned the rushing waters of the Swale for centuries, and it still carries the main B6270 valley road today.

◀ **Gayle**
The Village c1950 G345005
The pretty village of Gayle lies just to the south of Hawes in central Wensleydale, at the entrance to the little-frequented valley of Sleddale. Like many Dales villages, it is has a set of waterfalls, which we see here tumbling over the raised shelves of limestone. Note the old-fashioned traffic signs in the village street.

◀ **Grinton
General View c1960**
G62007
A general view of
Grinton, on the south
bank of the River Swale
nine miles west of
Richmond in Swaledale.
The sturdy bridge over
the Swale can be seen in
the centre of the
photograph, with the
brooding fells rising
beyond.

Gilling West
The War Memorial
c1955 G8303

Two cyclists - probably local men, judging from their flat caps - cycle past Gilling West's war memorial on the green of this small village just to the north of Richmond at the entrance to Swaledale in this timeless scene.

Grinton
St Andrew's Church,
the Norman Font
1913 65511

The Norman font at the west end of the parish church of St Andrews at Grinton has an ornately-carved wooden cover dating from the 15th century hanging above. The solidly-moulded tower arch in the background also dates from the 15th century.

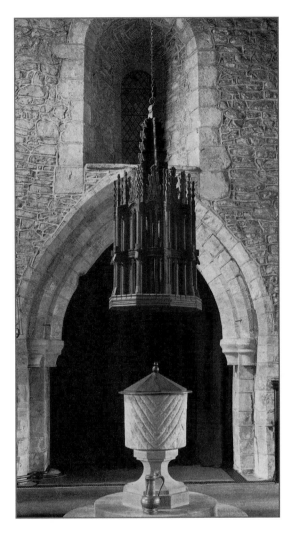

Gunnerside
The Bridge 1923 74373

Gunnerside lies in the heart of Swaledale. It is a village once famous for its lead mines, and the remains of many of them still survive in the gills and becks of the surrounding fells. This graceful, inclining bridge crosses the powerful waters of the Swale to the south of the village.

Hawes
The Street 1900

45633

The bustling village of Hawes is the 'capital' of Upper Wensleydale, and its main street is the economic and social centre for the farmers of the dale. Note the horse harnesses hanging outside the saddlers' shop in the left centre of the photograph.

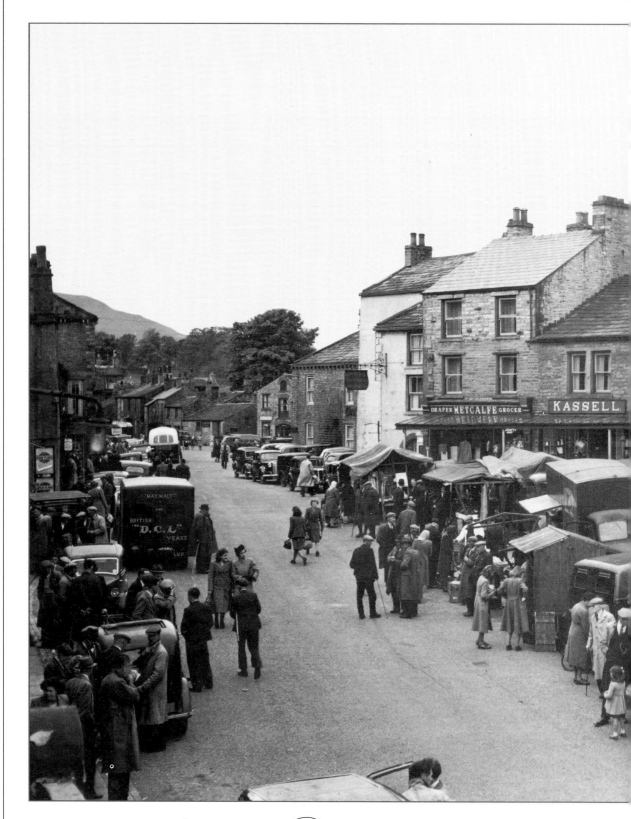

Hawes
The Main Street
c1955 H44001
This view of market day looks in the opposite direction from picture 45633 (pages 74-75). It shows Hawes's main street packed with visitors, farmers and their wives. Hawes is famous for its Wensleydale cheese and thanks to a successful local campaign to keep it open, it still has an active dairy producing the crumbly delicacy.

Hawes, Haymaking 1924 75754
The farmer with the horse-drawn 'sled' watches as two
women workers rake the hay. In the background is the parish
church of St Margaret's, built around 1850 after the
demolition of an older chapel.

Hawes, Ghyll Farm 1911 63489
Ghyll Farm, near Hawes, is a typically isolated Dales farmstead which probably dates back to the time of the first Norse settlers in Wensleydale. Ghyll or gill is an Old Norse name meaning a ravine or narrow valley, a precise description of the watercourse in the foreground of this picture.

Hawes, The Flagged Path to Hardraw 1925 77857
This stone-flagged path leads through a 'squeezer' stile in the foreground and across the fields towards Hardraw to the north, passing a typical Dales barn in the middle distance. This path is now followed by the Pennine Way long-distance footpath.

◄ **Healaugh
General View c1955**
H196004
Healaugh is a Swaledale village between Reeth and Gunnerside, situated where the Barney Beck enters the dale from the north. This general view shows the broad pasture meadows of the valley floor.

◀ **Hawes**
Stagsfell 1924 75757
A herd of Shorthorn cows graze peacefully in the meadows above Hawes in Wensleydale, with the heights of Stag's Fell rising across the River Ure beyond to the north. Note the pattern of dry stone walls spreading across this typical Yorkshire Dales landscape.

▼ **Healaugh**
The Lock Heather Guest House c1955 H196013
By the mid-Fifties, tourism was starting to occupy a much more important position in the Dales economy, alongside the traditional industries of farming and lead mining. The Lock Heather Guest House, with its pillar-type postbox outside the front gate, is an indication of changing times.

◀ **Jervaulx Abbey 1893**
33125
The picturesque ruins of Jervaulx Abbey lie in the grounds of Jervaulx Hall between Masham and Leyburn in Wensleydale. Founded in 1156, it housed monks of the Cistercian order and lasted for 400 years until it was demolished after the Dissolution in 1539.

Keld
Swaledale from West
Keld c1935 K66007
The circuitous narrow road which leads up from the Swaledale village of Keld is negotiated by an early motorcar. In the background behind the car we can see the River Swale, here in its higher and wilder reaches.

Keld
Swinner Gill Kirk c1940
K66014

Swinner Gill Kirk is a natural amphitheatre of rocks over which the Hind Hole Beck cascades, to the east of Keld and across the Swale on its northern bank. The name 'kirk' is significant, because it is the Old Norse name for a village with a church, and this must have seemed like a natural cathedral.

▼ **Keld, General View c1940** K66015

Keld lies in the background to the right in this view of the village from across the footbridge (centre left) over the river, which is now used by the Pennine Way long distance path.

▲ **Leyburn**
From the Church
Tower 1893 33113

Leyburn, at the eastern end of Wensleydale, boasts no less than three squares, the largest being the sloping rectangular Market Place which can be seen in the distance in this view from the tower of the village church. A weekly market is still held here on a Friday, as it has been since its charter was granted in 1686.

◀ **Leyburn**
The Moor Road to
Richmond 1924 75691
The moorland road via
Bellerby and Bardon Moor
runs north from Leyburn to
Richmond in Swaledale.
Isolated farmsteads, like
those seen in the middle
distance, dot its circuitous
route.

◀ **Low Row**
Looking East c1960
L169050
This photograph looks east down the broad, U-shaped valley of Swaledale from the oddly-named village of Low Row. The name comes from the fact that it is a linear village strung out along the valley road which runs close to the river on the northern side of the dale.

◄ **Low Row**
Whita Bridge c1955
L169011
Whita Bridge crosses the River Swale at Low Whita, a mile and a half downstream from the mid-Swaledale village of Low Row. It is a sturdy, three-arched structure which carries a steep minor road south over the moors to Askrigg in Wensleydale.

▼ **Low Row**
The Punch Bowl Inn c1960 L169054
Empty beer barrels await collection outside the barn alongside the Punch Bowl Inn in Low Row. The three-storied structure is a prominent feature in the centre of this mile-long linear Swaledale village.

◄ **Marske**
The Village 1913 65524
Marske, on the northern bank of the Swale as it approaches Richmond, is a more a collection of scattered farms than a village, as seen in this photograph. The wooded slopes of Dee Park Wood watch over the scattered settlement.

◄ **Marske**
Clints Cottage and the
Chapel c1955 M378006
The apse-ended chapel
on the village green in
the centre of Marske is
another example of the
strength of the non-
Conformist faith in the
former lead mining
villages of Swaledale.

◄ **Marske**
The Village c1955 M378003
The former Temperance Hotel in the centre of Marske, now Temperance Farm, was originally the Dormouse Inn. It changed its name after a Bonfire Night riot by carters in the early years of the 20th century and became one of the many non-alcoholic temperance hotels which were once a common feature of non-Conformist northern villages. Today they are few and far between.

▼ **Marske**
The Hall c1896 4709
Jacobean Marske Hall was the former home of the Hutton family, prominent landowners in this part of Swaledale. The prominent, triple-turreted and pantiled-roofed building is now used for local housing and is divided up into flats.

◄ **Masham**
From The Grotto 1908
60694
The spire of St Mary's parish church dominates this view, with the weir in the River Ure prominent in the foreground. Masham is perhaps best-known for Theakstone's Brewery, famous for its potent 'Old Peculier' beer.

**Masham
The Church 1927**
80262
The lower part of the
tower of St Mary's,
Masham, which is
seen here from the
spacious Market Place,
is 11th-century. But the
elegant octagonal-based
spire was added during
the 15th century, and is
a landmark for miles
around.

▼ **Masham, The Druids' Temple c1960** M45054
This miniature model of Stonehenge in far-off Wiltshire was erected by William Danby of Swinton Hall, Ilton, near Masham in around 1820 as a folly to interest and impress visitors to his estate. The strange monolith seen through the trilithon in the centre of the photograph bears no resemblance to any Neolithic monument, however.

▼ **Middleham, The Castle 1893** 33128
Middleham's massive castle overlooking the lower reaches of Wensleydale dates from the 11th century, and was once the home of Richard, Duke of York, who later became King Richard III. This view is from the south-east.

▲ **Middleham East Witton Road 1914**
67197
Good stabling was still being advertised at the Black Bull Hotel on the East Witton Road at Middleham when this photograph was taken. Note the man with the wheelbarrow in the middle distance - he seems to be clearing up some of the remains left by the horses using the stabling!

◄ **Middleham**
West End 1914 67201
The west end of Middleham
has some fine Georgian
terraced cottages. Note the
gas street lamp on the
right-hand end, and the
battlements on the end wall,
above the Edwardian lady
standing in the doorway.
A man with horse and cart
stands on the left.

Middleham, The Cover Bridge 1911 63447
The Cover Bridge at Middleham echoes the towers and battlements of
the castle. A horse and cart stand waiting in the middle of the bridge.

Middleham, Racehorses on the Moor 1914 67200d
In addition to its castle, Middleham is famous for its racehorses, and this photograph of the Low Moor shows a string of horses ridden by flat-capped jockeys walking in a wide circle with the trainer supervising in the middle.

Middleton Tyas, The Green c1960 M73009
Not truly in the Dales, Middleton Tyas lies a mile to the east of Scotch Corner, the famous junction on the A1 Great North Road. This photograph shows a pleasant range of pantiled cottages on the village green.

▼ **Middleton Tyas, The Scotch Corner Hotel c1960** M73014
A landmark to motorists for many years, the huge Scotch Corner
Hotel on the Great North Road at Middleton Tyas stands near the
junction of the A1 and the A66 cross-Pennine Stainmore road to
Penrith in Cumbria.

▼ **Newbiggin, The Cross Roads c1955** N256005
Newbiggin is a small village in Bishopdale, to the south of Aysgarth,
and its crossroads is an important village landmark. The dale road
from Kettlewell in Wharfedale and the minor road through Thoralby to
Aysgarth intersect here.

▲ **Ravensworth
The Castle c1913** 65497
The ruinous remains of
Sir Henry Fitzhugh's
14th-century castle lie to
the south-east of the
small village of
Ravensworth, in the
'forgotten dale' of
Holmedale to the north of
Richmond. There is
believed to have been an
earlier Norman castle on
the site.

◄ **Redmire**
The Village 1929 82584
Redmire is a tidy village in mid-Wensleydale. In the left background we can just see the Bolton Arms, a popular village hostelry which recalls the name of a prominent local family.

◀ **Reeth**
From the South 1913
65530
Reeth stands at the confluence of the River Swale and the Arkle Beck, and it is the largest village in mid-Swaledale. This view from the south shows its greystone cottages growing almost organically from the surrounding fells.

Redmire
The Village and the Post Office 1929 82589
Taken on the same day as photograph 82584, this view of Redmire shows the village green with two horse-drawn carts loaded with hay under the tree in the left background. The village Post Office is on the left. Most of the railed trees on the green were planted to mark coronations and royal jubilees.

Reeth
General View 1913 65528
The centre of Reeth as it looked just before the outbreak of the First World War. Note the absence of traffic of any kind, the solid Victorian and Georgian cottages, including the Post Office (with public telephone), and the Georgian-windowed Wesleyan Chapel on the extreme right.

Reeth
The Green c1955
R238004
Note the variety of wooden seats provided for people to sit and admire the scene, the fine range of buildings, and the ancient Bedford bus on the extreme left, in front of the white-painted Black Bull Hotel.

Reeth
The Village 1923 74363
This view of the village
shows its spacious green,
where the famous Bartle
Fairs (named after
St Bartholomew's Day)
were held from the late
17th century. Reeth's
green is typical of those
in many Pennine villages
where cattle were herded
in times of trouble, with
the cottages grouped
protectively around it.

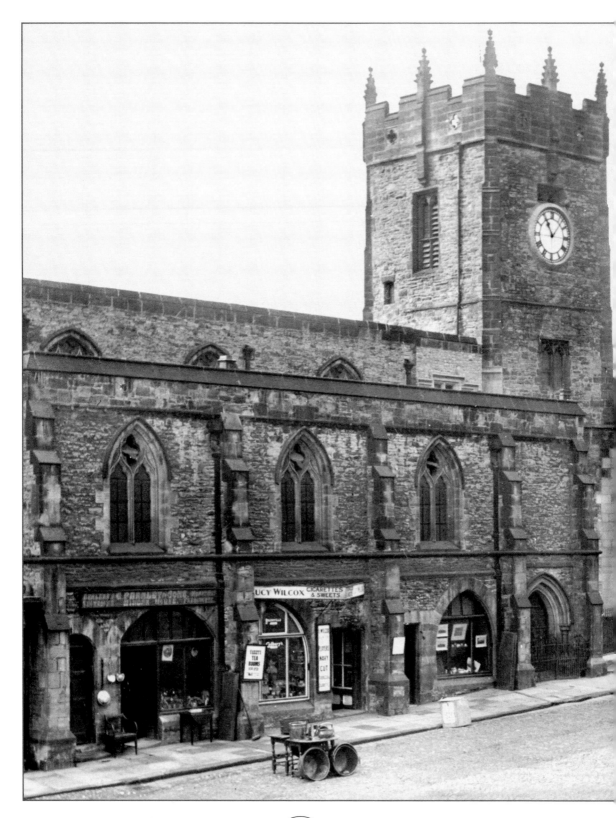

Richmond
The Market Place
1929 82555
Holy Trinity church, Richmond, was unlike any other church in the country when this photograph was taken, because it had shops built into its northern walls. Later it was to become the museum of the Green Howards Regiment from nearby Catterick.

▼ **Richmond, From the North 1908** 59489

Richmond is the 'capital' of Swaledale and its largest town, situated at its eastern entrance. This view from the north shows most of the bustling little market town's main buildings: from right to left we see the Castle, Holy Trinity Church, and the tower of the parish church of St Mary.

▼ **Richmond, The Castle 1898** 41642

The towering walls of Richmond Castle have watched over the little Swaledale town for over 900 years. This view from Richmond Green shows the towering Norman keep, one of the best-preserved in England, on the left, and the ivy-clad curtain walls on the prominent crag which looks down on the town and river beneath.

▲ **Richmond
The Castle and the
Bridge 1929** 82540
Another view of Richmond Castle, this time from the river and showing the Green Bridge, one of two which cross the mighty Swale. The strong defensive nature of the castle's situation is well shown here.

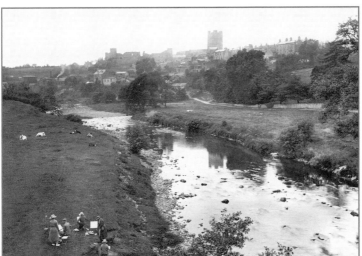

◀ **Richmond
From the River 1923**
74348
A group of Edwardian lady artists, in the left foreground, chose a superb site to paint this distant view of Richmond from the banks of the River Swale. As usual with views of Richmond, the castle is prominent on the skyline, and reflected in the waters of the river.

Richmond, The Falls 1913 65534
The River Swale runs over a series of stepped, weir-like waterfalls just upstream from Richmond, where the river enters a pleasantly-wooded gorge.

Scorton, The Village c1960 S75009
An apron-clad mother leads her small son by the hand through the main street of Scorton, across the A1 from Catterick, in this charming photograph. Perhaps they were going to R Gaskell's grocery shop, seen on the extreme right of the picture.

Semer Water, The Foot of the Lake 1911 63501
Semer Water, the largest natural lake in Yorkshire, seen from the
Carlow Stone, a glacial erratic. Yorkshire being a county of
superlatives, Semer Water is drained by England's shortest river,
the Bain, which runs into Wensleydale at Bainbridge.

Semer Water 1929
82610
A peaceful view of two boats tied up and waiting for visitors in the shallows of Semer Water. Semer Water, which is about half a mile in length and covers about 100 acres, was formed by Ice Age glaciers forming in the side dale known as Raydale.

◀ **Swaledale
Hudswell Bank 1913**
65516
Looking west up the dale,
upstream from Richmond,
Hudswell Bank's woodlands
are now in the care of the
National Trust, and offer
some good, sheltered walks
and fine views across
Swaledale.

◀ **Swaledale 1924** 75742
This is the archetypal view of a Yorkshire Dale, in this case Swaledale, perhaps the least spoiled of them all. It shows a U-shaped valley formed by the glaciers of the Ice Age, a typical Dales stone-built barn on the left, built to take the summer's hay for winter feed, and the network of dry stone walls sweeping down to the valley floor with the high moorland above.

▼ **Swaledale
The View from Kisdon Foss 1896** 38297
This view looks downstream down the gorge of the River Swale from the top of Kisdon Foss (or Force) near Keld in Upper Swaledale. Here the river is forced into a narrow channel between the Birk and Beldi Hills, the last of which gave its name to a lead mine on the hills above.

◀ **Tanhill
The Tan Hill Inn
c1955** T351003
The Tan Hill Inn, occupying a desolate moorland location at 1,732ft on Sleightholme Moor between Swaledale and the valley of the Greta to the north, is well known as the highest inn in England. For many years, it was the site of an annual sheep sale; today it is a welcome refreshment stop for walkers on the Pennine Way.

◀ **Thwaite
The Village and
Buttertubs Pass c1960**
T135012
The Cliff Gate Road
winds up from Thwaite
village, seen here in the
bottom of the picture,
and rises to 1,725 feet
at the remote Buttertubs
Pass, and links Thwaite
in Swaledale to Hawes in
Wensleydale to the
south.

◀ **Thwaite**
The Bridge c1960

T135005

The ancient bridge over the Thwaite Beck stands in the centre of this small village at the foot of Kisdon Hill in Swaledale. It is perhaps best known as the birthplace of the Kearton brothers, Richard and Cherry, pioneer naturalists and wildlife photographers.

▼ **Thwaite**
The Buttertubs 1908

60806A

The Buttertubs Pass takes its name from these strange, circular 100-foot deep fissures or pot holes in the limestone, which are said to resemble the wooden tubs in which butter used to be stored. Shade-loving ferns such as hart's tongue thrive in their vertiginous depths.

◀ **West Burton**
The Bridge and the Falls 1893 33146

A Victorian lady in a long dress stands on the banks of the Walden Beck by the packhorse bridge just below the village of West Burton, which is situated just south of Wensleydale at the junction of Bishopsdale and the valley of the Walden.

West Burton, The Village 1914 67211
The centrepiece of West Burton is this stepped obelisk, dated 1802, standing on the village green. A pony grazes to the right of the landmark, and the greystone cottages, now part of a Conservation Area, cluster around the greensward.

West Witton, The Village 1911 63451
A general view of West Witton, which stands at the eastern entrance to Wensleydale. West Witton lies in the shadow of Pen Hill on the southern side of the dale. In the far distance we can just see the 16th-century tower of the parish church of St Bartholomew.

Index

Frith Book Co Titles

www.francisfrith.co.uk

The Frith Book Company publishes over 100 new titles each year. A selection of those currently available are listed below. For latest catalogue please contact Frith Book Co.

Town Books 96 pages, approx 100 photos. County and Themed Books 128 pages, approx 150 photos (unless specified). All titles hardback laminated case and jacket except those indicated pb (paperback)

Amersham, Chesham & Rickmansworth (pb)	1-85937-340-2	£9.99
Ancient Monuments & Stone Circles	1-85937-143-4	£17.99
Aylesbury (pb)	1-85937-227-9	£9.99
Bakewell	1-85937-113-2	£12.99
Barnstaple (pb)	1-85937-300-3	£9.99
Bath (pb)	1-85937419-0	£9.99
Bedford (pb)	1-85937-205-8	£9.99
Berkshire (pb)	1-85937-191-4	£9.99
Berkshire Churches	1-85937-170-1	£17.99
Blackpool (pb)	1-85937-382-8	£9.99
Bognor Regis (pb)	1-85937-431-x	£9.99
Bournemouth	1-85937-067-5	£12.99
Bradford (pb)	1-85937-204-x	£9.99
Brighton & Hove(pb)	1-85937-192-2	£8.99
Bristol (pb)	1-85937-264-3	£9.99
British Life A Century Ago (pb)	1-85937-213-9	£9.99
Buckinghamshire (pb)	1-85937-200-7	£9.99
Camberley (pb)	1-85937-222-8	£9.99
Cambridge (pb)	1-85937-422-0	£9.99
Cambridgeshire (pb)	1-85937-420-4	£9.99
Canals & Waterways (pb)	1-85937-291-0	£9.99
Canterbury Cathedral (pb)	1-85937-179-5	£9.99
Cardiff (pb)	1-85937-093-4	£9.99
Carmarthenshire	1-85937-216-3	£14.99
Chelmsford (pb)	1-85937-310-0	£9.99
Cheltenham (pb)	1-85937-095-0	£9.99
Cheshire (pb)	1-85937-271-6	£9.99
Chester	1-85937-090-x	£12.99
Chesterfield	1-85937-378-x	£9.99
Chichester (pb)	1-85937-228-7	£9.99
Colchester (pb)	1-85937-188-4	£8.99
Cornish Coast	1-85937-163-9	£14.99
Cornwall (pb)	1-85937-229-5	£9.99
Cornwall Living Memories	1-85937-248-1	£14.99
Cotswolds (pb)	1-85937-230-9	£9.99
Cotswolds Living Memories	1-85937-255-4	£14.99
County Durham	1-85937-123-x	£14.99
Croydon Living Memories	1-85937-162-0	£9.99
Cumbria	1-85937-101-9	£14.99
Dartmoor	1-85937-145-0	£14.99
Derby (pb)	1-85937-367-4	£9.99
Derbyshire (pb)	1-85937-196-5	£9.99
Devon (pb)	1-85937-297-x	£9.99
Dorset (pb)	1-85937-269-4	£9.99
Dorset Churches	1-85937-172-8	£17.99
Dorset Coast (pb)	1-85937-299-6	£9.99
Dorset Living Memories	1-85937-210-4	£14.99
Down the Severn	1-85937-118-3	£14.99
Down the Thames (pb)	1-85937-278-3	£9.99
Down the Trent	1-85937-311-9	£14.99
Dublin (pb)	1-85937-231-7	£9.99
East Anglia (pb)	1-85937-265-1	£9.99
East London	1-85937-080-2	£14.99
East Sussex	1-85937-130-2	£14.99
Eastbourne	1-85937-061-6	£12.99
Edinburgh (pb)	1-85937-193-0	£8.99
England in the 1880s	1-85937-331-3	£17.99
English Castles (pb)	1-85937-434-4	£9.99
English Country Houses	1-85937-161-2	£17.99
Essex (pb)	1-85937-270-8	£9.99
Exeter	1-85937-126-4	£12.99
Exmoor	1-85937-132-9	£14.99
Falmouth	1-85937-066-7	£12.99
Folkestone (pb)	1-85937-124-8	£9.99
Glasgow (pb)	1-85937-190-6	£9.99
Gloucestershire	1-85937-102-7	£14.99
Great Yarmouth (pb)	1-85937-426-3	£9.99
Greater Manchester (pb)	1-85937-266-x	£9.99
Guildford (pb)	1-85937-410-7	£9.99
Hampshire (pb)	1-85937-279-1	£9.99
Hampshire Churches (pb)	1-85937-207-4	£9.99
Harrogate	1-85937-423-9	£9.99
Hastings & Bexhill (pb)	1-85937-131-0	£9.99
Heart of Lancashire (pb)	1-85937-197-3	£9.99
Helston (pb)	1-85937-214-7	£9.99
Hereford (pb)	1-85937-175-2	£9.99
Herefordshire	1-85937-174-4	£14.99
Hertfordshire (pb)	1-85937-247-3	£9.99
Horsham (pb)	1-85937-432-8	£9.99
Humberside	1-85937-215-5	£14.99
Hythe, Romney Marsh & Ashford	1-85937-256-2	£9.99

Available from your local bookshop or from the publisher

Title	ISBN	Price	Title	ISBN	Price
Ipswich (pb)	1-85937-424-7	£9.99	St Ives (pb)	1-85937415-8	£9.99
Ireland (pb)	1-85937-181-7	£9.99	Scotland (pb)	1-85937-182-5	£9.99
Isle of Man (pb)	1-85937-268-6	£9.99	Scottish Castles (pb)	1-85937-323-2	£9.99
Isles of Scilly	1-85937-136-1	£14.99	Sevenoaks & Tunbridge	1-85937-057-8	£12.99
Isle of Wight (pb)	1-85937-429-8	£9.99	Sheffield, South Yorks (pb)	1-85937-267-8	£9.99
Isle of Wight Living Memories	1-85937-304-6	£14.99	Shrewsbury (pb)	1-85937-325-9	£9.99
Kent (pb)	1-85937-189-2	£9.99	Shropshire (pb)	1-85937-326-7	£9.99
Kent Living Memories	1-85937-125-6	£14.99	Somerset	1-85937-153-1	£14.99
Lake District (pb)	1-85937-275-9	£9.99	South Devon Coast	1-85937-107-8	£14.99
Lancaster, Morecambe & Heysham (pb)	1-85937-233-3	£9.99	South Devon Living Memories	1-85937-168-x	£14.99
Leeds (pb)	1-85937-202-3	£9.99	South Hams	1-85937-220-1	£14.99
Leicester	1-85937-073-x	£12.99	Southampton (pb)	1-85937-427-1	£9.99
Leicestershire (pb)	1-85937-185-x	£9.99	Southport (pb)	1-85937-425-5	£9.99
Lincolnshire (pb)	1-85937-433-6	£9.99	Staffordshire	1-85937-047-0	£12.99
Liverpool & Merseyside (pb)	1-85937-234-1	£9.99	Stratford upon Avon	1-85937-098-5	£12.99
London (pb)	1-85937-183-3	£9.99	Suffolk (pb)	1-85937-221-x	£9.99
Ludlow (pb)	1-85937-176-0	£9.99	Suffolk Coast	1-85937-259-7	£14.99
Luton (pb)	1-85937-235-x	£9.99	Surrey (pb)	1-85937-240-6	£9.99
Maidstone	1-85937-056-x	£14.99	Sussex (pb)	1-85937-184-1	£9.99
Manchester (pb)	1-85937-198-1	£9.99	Swansea (pb)	1-85937-167-1	£9.99
Middlesex	1-85937-158-2	£14.99	Tees Valley & Cleveland	1-85937-211-2	£14.99
New Forest	1-85937-128-0	£14.99	Thanet (pb)	1-85937-116-7	£9.99
Newark (pb)	1-85937-366-6	£9.99	Tiverton (pb)	1-85937-178-7	£9.99
Newport, Wales (pb)	1-85937-258-9	£9.99	Torbay	1-85937-063-2	£12.99
Newquay (pb)	1-85937-421-2	£9.99	Truro	1-85937-147-7	£12.99
Norfolk (pb)	1-85937-195-7	£9.99	Victorian and Edwardian Cornwall	1-85937-252-x	£14.99
Norfolk Living Memories	1-85937-217-1	£14.99	Victorian & Edwardian Devon	1-85937-253-8	£14.99
Northamptonshire	1-85937-150-7	£14.99	Victorian & Edwardian Kent	1-85937-149-3	£14.99
Northumberland Tyne & Wear (pb)	1-85937-281-3	£9.99	Vic & Ed Maritime Album	1-85937-144-2	£17.99
North Devon Coast	1-85937-146-9	£14.99	Victorian and Edwardian Sussex	1-85937-157-4	£14.99
North Devon Living Memories	1-85937-261-9	£14.99	Victorian & Edwardian Yorkshire	1-85937-154-x	£14.99
North London	1-85937-206-6	£14.99	Victorian Seaside	1-85937-159-0	£17.99
North Wales (pb)	1-85937-298-8	£9.99	Villages of Devon (pb)	1-85937-293-7	£9.99
North Yorkshire (pb)	1-85937-236-8	£9.99	Villages of Kent (pb)	1-85937-294-5	£9.99
Norwich (pb)	1-85937-194-9	£8.99	Villages of Sussex (pb)	1-85937-295-3	£9.99
Nottingham (pb)	1-85937-324-0	£9.99	Warwickshire (pb)	1-85937-203-1	£9.99
Nottinghamshire (pb)	1-85937-187-6	£9.99	Welsh Castles (pb)	1-85937-322-4	£9.99
Oxford (pb)	1-85937-411-5	£9.99	West Midlands (pb)	1-85937-289-9	£9.99
Oxfordshire (pb)	1-85937-430-1	£9.99	West Sussex	1-85937-148-5	£14.99
Peak District (pb)	1-85937-280-5	£9.99	West Yorkshire (pb)	1-85937-201-5	£9.99
Penzance	1-85937-069-1	£12.99	Weymouth (pb)	1-85937-209-0	£9.99
Peterborough (pb)	1-85937-219-8	£9.99	Wiltshire (pb)	1-85937-277-5	£9.99
Piers	1-85937-237-6	£17.99	Wiltshire Churches (pb)	1-85937-171-x	£9.99
Plymouth	1-85937-119-1	£12.99	Wiltshire Living Memories	1-85937-245-7	£14.99
Poole & Sandbanks (pb)	1-85937-251-1	£9.99	Winchester (pb)	1-85937-428-x	£9.99
Preston (pb)	1-85937-212-0	£9.99	Windmills & Watermills	1-85937-242-2	£17.99
Reading (pb)	1-85937-238-4	£9.99	Worcester (pb)	1-85937-165-5	£9.99
Romford (pb)	1-85937-319-4	£9.99	Worcestershire	1-85937-152-3	£14.99
Salisbury (pb)	1-85937-239-2	£9.99	York (pb)	1-85937-199-x	£9.99
Scarborough (pb)	1-85937-379-8	£9.99	Yorkshire (pb)	1-85937-186-8	£9.99
St Albans (pb)	1-85937-341-0	£9.99	Yorkshire Living Memories	1-85937-166-3	£14.99

See Frith books on the internet www.francisfrith.co.uk

FRITH PRODUCTS & SERVICES

Francis Frith would doubtless be pleased to know that the pioneering publishing venture he started in 1860 still continues today. A hundred and forty years later, The Francis Frith Collection continues in the same innovative tradition and is now one of the foremost publishers of vintage photographs in the world. Some of the current activities include:

Interior Decoration

Today Frith's photographs can be seen framed and as giant wall murals in thousands of pubs, restaurants, hotels, banks, retail stores and other public buildings throughout the country. In every case they enhance the unique local atmosphere of the places they depict and provide reminders of gentler days in an increasingly busy and frenetic world.

Product Promotions

Frith products are used by many major companies to promote the sales of their own products or to reinforce their own history and heritage. Frith promotions have been used by Hovis bread, Courage beers, Scots Porage Oats, Colman's mustard, Cadbury's foods, Mellow Birds coffee, Dunhill pipe tobacco, Guinness, and Bulmer's Cider.

Genealogy and Family History

As the interest in family history and roots grows world-wide, more and more people are turning to Frith's photographs of Great Britain for images of the towns, villages and streets where their ancestors lived; and, of course, photographs of the churches and chapels where their ancestors were christened, married and buried are an essential part of every genealogy tree and family album.

Frith Products

All Frith photographs are available Framed or just as Mounted Prints and Posters (size 23 x 16 inches). These may be ordered from the address below. From time to time other products - Address Books, Calendars, Table Mats, etc - are available.

The Internet

Already twenty thousand Frith photographs can be viewed and purchased on the internet through the Frith websites and a myriad of partner sites.

For more detailed information on Frith companies and products, look at these sites:

www.francisfrith.co.uk
www.francisfrith.com
(for North American visitors)

See the complete list of Frith Books at:
www.francisfrith.co.uk
This web site is regularly updated with the latest list of publications from the Frith Book Company. If you wish to buy books relating to another part of the country that your local bookshop does not stock, you may purchase on-line.

For further information, trade, or author enquiries please contact us at the address below:
The Francis Frith Collection, Frith's Barn, Teffont, Salisbury, Wiltshire, England SP3 5QP.
Tel: +44 (0)1722 716 376 Fax: +44 (0)1722 716 881 Email: sales@francisfrith.co.uk

See Frith books on the internet www.francisfrith.co.uk

TO RECEIVE YOUR FREE MOUNTED PRINT

Mounted Print
Overall size 14 x 11 inches

Cut out this Voucher and return it with your remittance for £1.95 to cover postage and handling, to UK addresses. For overseas addresses please include £4.00 post and handling. Choose any photograph included in this book. Your SEPIA print will be A4 in size, and mounted in a cream mount with burgundy rule line, overall size 14 x 11 inches.

Order additional Mounted Prints at HALF PRICE (only £7.49 each*)

If there are further pictures you would like to order, possibly as gifts for friends and family, purchase them at half price (no additional postage and handling required).

Have your Mounted Prints framed*

For an additional £14.95 per print you can have your chosen Mounted Print framed in an elegant polished wood and gilt moulding, overall size 16 x 13 inches (no additional postage and handling required).

---

* IMPORTANT!
These special prices are only available if ordered using the original voucher on this page (no copies permitted) and at the same time as your free Mounted Print, for delivery to the same address

---

Frith Collectors' Guild

From time to time we publish a magazine of news and stories about Frith photographs and further special offers of Frith products. If you would like 12 months FREE membership, please return this form.

Send completed forms to:
**The Francis Frith Collection,
Frith's Barn, Teffont, Salisbury,
Wiltshire SP3 5QP**

Voucher for FREE and Reduced Price Frith Prints

Picture no.	Page number	Qty	Mounted @ £7.49	Framed + £14.95	Total Cost
		1	**Free of charge***	£	£
			£7.49	£	£
			£7.49	£	£
			£7.49	£	£
			£7.49	£	£
			£7.49	£	£

Please allow 28 days for delivery	*** Post & handling**	**£1.95**
Book Title	**Total Order Cost**	**£**

Please do not photocopy this voucher. Only the original is valid, so please cut it out and return it to us.

I enclose a cheque / postal order for £ . . . .
made payable to 'The Francis Frith Collection'
OR please debit my Mastercard / Visa / Switch / Amex card
(credit cards please on all overseas orders)

Number . . . .

Issue No(Switch only) . . . . .Valid from (Amex/Switch) . . . .

Expires . . . . Signature . . . .

Name Mr/Mrs/Ms . . . .

Address . . . .

. . . .

. . . .

. . . . Postcode . . . .

Daytime Tel No . . . .   Valid to 31/12/03

The Francis Frith Collectors' Guild

Please enrol me as a member for 12 months free of charge.

Name Mr/Mrs/Ms . . . .

Address . . . .

. . . .

. . . .

. . . . Postcode . . . .

Would you like to find out more about Francis Frith?

We have recently recruited some entertaining speakers who are happy to visit local groups, clubs and societies to give an illustrated talk documenting Frith's travels and photographs. If you are a member of such a group and are interested in hosting a presentation, we would love to hear from you.

Our speakers bring with them a small selection of our local town and county books, together with sample prints. They are happy to take orders. A small proportion of the order value is donated to the group who have hosted the presentation. The talks are therefore an excellent way of fundraising for small groups and societies.

Can you help us with information about any of the Frith photographs in this book?

We are gradually compiling an historical record for each of the photographs in the Frith archive. It is always fascinating to find out the names of the people shown in the pictures, as well as insights into the shops, buildings and other features depicted.

If you recognize anyone in the photographs in this book, or if you have information not already included in the author's caption, do let us know. We would love to hear from you, and will try to publish it in future books or articles.

Our production team

Frith books are produced by a small dedicated team at offices in the converted Grade II listed 18th-century barn at Teffont near Salisbury, illustrated above. Most have worked with the Frith Collection for many years. All have in common one quality: they have a passion for the Frith Collection. The team is constantly expanding, but currently includes:

Jason Buck, John Buck, Douglas Burns, Heather Crisp, Lucy Elcock, Isobel Hall, Rob Hames, Hazel Heaton, Peter Horne, James Kinnear, Tina Leary, Hannah Marsh, Eliza Sackett, Terence Sackett, Sandra Sanger, Lewis Taylor, Shelley Tolcher, Helen Vimpany, Clive Wathen and Jenny Wathen.